Kevin Brophy and Jules Ober

Rockpooling

With Pup

Hello, I'm Mia and this is Pup.
Because we are very tiny, our adventures are extra big.
Come with us and explore the world that's at your feet!

The tide is out, so it's the perfect time to explore the rocky shore.

We can meet the creatures who live their lives there, pushed and pulled between the sand and the sea.

Let's follow that sea star — she's heading for the rock pools too.

What can we see here?

It might be an octopus's garden.

It is! Here she is — a blue-ringed octopus.

But where are her electric blue rings? She looks sad without them.

With my eyes that hardly ever close and Pup's super sniffing plastic nose,

we should search for those rings, and bring them back
before the tide comes in.

Hi Mr Crab, my name is Mia, and I'm on a quest. Have you seen any rings that are blue and lost?

No, no, not here snap-snap, snip-snip.
Look for the pool where the sea stars hide.

What have you found, clever Pup?
That's a blue ring all right, but it definitely doesn't belong here.

Hello sea stars. You've kept your blue.
You look just like my grandma's carpet.

Here's the sea urchin, balancing stones as she sings to herself in her pool. Look carefully — there are tiny glowing rings on her spines.

And here are some very strange rings, tightly closed and waiting for waves.
Would the octopus want to wear these?

We’ll have to go further. Down to the edge where the waves flick and spin,

and the kelp holds on tight to the rocks.

Careful! We'll follow this lumpy bumpy path.

Watch your nose, Pup. Those anemones will sting it if you get too close!

The pools are deeper and darker down here.

I wonder what that could be?

Look, those sea stars are having a party! There's dancing . . .

. . . and raspberry jelly. Or is that an outside-in anemone hiding in the beads of Neptune's necklace?

This looks like a lolly shop,

but everything's salty and slimy. Would you take a bite?

Um, hello! You seem to have a mouth.
Please tell us where we might find some electric blue rings?

All we've seen so far are tentacles, beaks, and snaily shells in slithery slime.

Here's the chiton. Surely with its one hundred eyes it has spied some pretty rings belonging to the octopus?

Wait up, Pup. What's the rush?
Nobody is telling us anything.

Follow your dog, little creature. He's sensing the rising tide.

Thanks hermit crab. I'm right behind you, Pup!

No stopping and wagging now, no lifting your ears.
Enough peering into magical pools.

We must go straight back to the octopus and tell her that we couldn't find her rings.

Pup has found her . . .

. . . and look! she's wearing her beautiful rings!

Quark! Quark! Keep your hands and paws out of her pool.
Those rings flash a warning!

Her nine octopus brains make her smarter than you think.
She's letting you know that she'll bite you if she has to.

Cormorants are crabby old know-alls, but this one saved us from a big mistake. Your friendly wagging ways nearly ended in a poisonous bite!

But you did sense the rising tide, you clever dog.
Those waves would carry us away in a woosh.

Time to head home now. We've had a big enough adventure for one day.

We'll dream of the rock pools tonight.

MORE ABOUT THE ROCKPOOLS

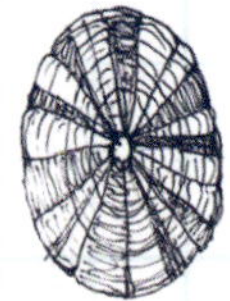

Limpets have a soft squishy body called a 'foot' that is covered by a hard shell like a tent. Their tongue, called a radula, is like a ribbon of teeth that scrapes delicious algae from the rocks.

The only thing a zebra snail has in common with a zebra is its black and white stripes.

The octopus has nine brains – one in its head and one in each of its eight arms. It can figure out how to open a shellfish with one arm while adding rocks and shells to its garden with another! The blue-ringed octopus is very poisonous, but it prefers to hide than to bite.

Neptune's necklace seaweed has beads that are filled with water to stop it from drying out, and air to make it float, so it can drift to new places but also catch the sun to convert light into food.

Swift-footed crabs can run really fast.
But they can't outrun the fact that as the ocean becomes warmer, it also becomes more acidic, which weakens the crab's shell making it brittle and more likely to break.

A sea star (not starfish – they aren't fish) has no brain and no blood, but if it loses an arm, it can grow another one! They live for up to 35 years, and some species have as many as 40 arms.

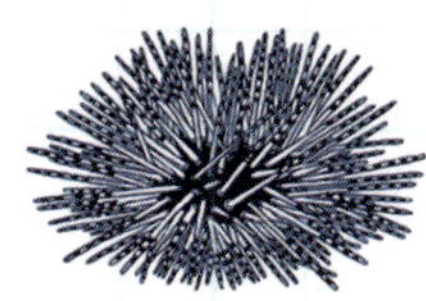

Sea urchins can live for up to 200 years! Their mouth is underneath their body and has five super strong teeth that can chew through rock, plus many tiny feet to enable them to walk around.

Anemones are the flowers of the sea, but don't sniff them because they are covered in stinging cells that paralyse their prey.
Anemones can clone themselves. If one half of the anemone walks west while the other half walks east, it can split.
There are now two anemones!

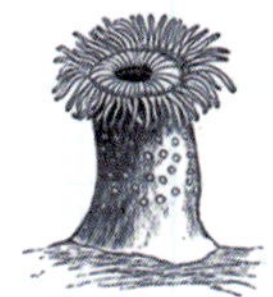

Acorn barnacles produce glue to stick themselves to rocks or whales or boats.
It's one of the strongest glues in the world!
Once they have attached themselves somewhere, they stay there for their whole life.

The Chiton is like a tiny tank covered with hundreds of invisible eyes made of the same stuff as its armour.

Hermit crabs live in groups and sometimes help each other.
They borrow shells from other creatures who no longer need them.
When a new shell becomes available, the little hermit crabs will line up to try it on.
The largest crab will try it first and if it's not big enough, the next crab will try it until the shell is a perfect fit for someone.

by Mia

Climate change is threatening life in the rock pools.
The delicate balance of each pool is upset by sea-level rise, warming waters and the increasing acidification of the oceans. As strengthening storms pound the coast, they further destabilise fragile marine habitats.

PLEASE DON'T TOUCH

The delicate balance of the rock pools can also be upset by things being touched and moved.
Stay safe on the rocks and help the creatures stay safe too.

TAKE ACTION TO PROTECT THE ROCK POOLS

Visit these websites to find out how:
Take 3 For the Sea **www.take3.org**
Aust. Marine Conservation Society **www.marineconservation.org.au**
Positive Change for Marine Life **www.pcfml.org.au**

PHOTOGRAPHED ON

the land of the Nuenonne, Lunawanna Allonah
the land of the Yaegl, Yuraygir NP
the land of the Yuin, Bermagui

THANKS TO

Dariia Pankova for 3D rendering the Mia doll.

Marine biologists **Anne Leitch** and **Andrew Page** for their careful watch over the facts.

Alex Mankiewicz and Tim-Jacques Ober for their ever thoughtful input.

Pierre-Jacques Ober for waiting patiently by the rock pools.

Elizabeth Hardaker for being a great snorkelling buddy.

DEDICATED TO

my daughter, **Solveig Ober** who inspired this story and my mum, **Wendy Harper** who introduced me to the rock pools as a little girl.

First published in 2022 by Ford Street Publishing, Melbourne, Victoria, Australia

2 4 6 8 10 9 7 5 3 1

Ford Street Publishing Pty Ltd,
162 Hoddle Street, Abbotsford, Vic 3067, Australia

ISBN 978-1-922696-13-7 (HB)

Printed in China by Tingleman Pty Ltd

www.fordstreetpublishing.com

A catalogue record for this book is available from the National Library of Australia